W9-ANU-101

What Do Critters Do in the Winter?

by Julie K. Lundgren

Science Content Editor:
Kristi Lew

www.rourkepublishing.com

Science content editor: Kristi Lew
A former high school teacher with a background in biochemistry and more than 10 years of experience in cytogenetic laboratories, Kristi Lew specializes in taking complex scientific information and making it fun and interesting for scientists and non-scientists alike. She is the author of more than 20 science books for children and teachers.

www.rourkepublishing.com

The author also thanks Melissa Martyr-Wagner and Sam, Riley and Steve Lundgren.

Photo credits: Cover © nialat; Table of Contents © Eric Isselée; Page 4/5 © riganmc; Page 6 © Eric Isselée; Page 7 © S.R. Maglione; Page 8 © Jordan McCullough; Page 9 © Gooddenka; Page 10 © © Kevin Dyer; Page 11 © Bruce MacQueen; Page 12 © Dennis Donohue; Page 13 © nialat; Page 14 © Studiotouch; Page 15 © nialat; Page 16 © Winthrop Brookhouse; Page 17 © Vladimir Chernyanskiy; Page 18 © Jordan McCullough; Page 19 © fotoret; Page 20 © Witold Kaszkin; Page 21 © Michael Woodruff

Editor: Kelli Hicks

Cover and page design by Nicola Stratford, bdpublishing.com

Library of Congress Cataloging-in-Publication Data

Lundgren, Julie K.
 What do critters do in the winter? / Julie K. Lundgren.
    p. cm. -- (My science library)
 Includes bibliographical references and index.
 ISBN 978-1-61741-746-7 (Hard cover) (alk. paper)
 ISBN 978-1-61741-948-5 (Soft cover)
 1. Animals--Wintering--Juvenile literature. 2. Hibernation--Juvenile literature. I. Title.
 QL753.L86 2012
 591.4'3--dc22
                              2011004759

Rourke Publishing
Printed in the United States of America,
North Mankato, Minnesota
060711
060711CL

www.rourkepublishing.com - rourke@rourkepublishing.com
Post Office Box 643328 Vero Beach, Florida 32964

Table of Contents

Cold, Snow, and Ice

In many parts of the world, winter brings cold temperatures, snow, and ice.

In winter, lakes freeze and snow covers the land.

5

Animals that live in places where seasons change have many **adaptations** to **survive** winter. Adaptations include ways animals look and how they act.

Many layers of thick fur keep wolves warm.

Winter Adaptations

How do animals survive winter? Many animals **migrate**, or move from one place to another. Animals with wings may migrate in the fall. Some **herd** animals, such as **caribou**, also migrate.

Many Monarch butterflies migrate to California and Mexico.

Some caribou herds migrate over 400 miles (644 kilometers) between their summer and winter homes.

Some animals **hibernate**. Many toads dig down into the soil and go into what seems like a long, deep sleep. Other hibernators eat heavily in the fall to get fat.

Some toads hibernate in burrows.

Since they cannot eat while they hibernate, they use **energy** from their body fat to stay alive.

Woodchucks, also known as groundhogs, eat constantly as the time to hibernate nears.

Other animals are not true hibernators, but they do spend much of the winter in their homes living on stored food and resting.

Skunks, raccoons, and black bears wake to eat on warmer days.

Raccoon

13

Active animals have other adaptations. Some animals' fur turns from brown to white for the winter months. This **camouflage** helps them blend in against the snow.

The snowshoe hare's fur coat helps it hide from its enemies in summer and in winter.

Many active animals eat stored food or grow thicker fur. Others, such as mice, live in tunnels under the snow. Snow acts like a blanket to help keep them warm.

Gray jays store insects, berries, seeds, and other foods in trees.

Rodents stay warm and hidden by using a network of snow tunnels.

Spring Again

As spring returns, temperatures rise and the snow and ice melt away. Migrating animals return.

Monarchs begin flying north in March.

Early flowers welcome spring.

19

Sleeping animals wake. Color changers replace their white fur with summer brown. The animals have used their adaptations to survive and are ready for spring.

In spring, the Arctic fox sheds its white winter fur and grows a lighter, brown coat.

For people in the northern United States and Canada, the robin's return is a sign of spring.

21

SHOW What You Know

1. How is winter hard for animals?

2. What adaptations do animals have for surviving winter?

3. Why do animals migrate?

Glossary

active (AK-tiv): to eat, move, rest, and live as usual

adaptations (ad-ap-TAY-shunz): ways animals change over time to help them survive, including changes in the way they look and act

camouflage (KAM-uh-flahzh): colorations that blend with the surroundings, to help animals stay hidden

caribou (KAIR-uh-boo): reindeer of North America

energy (en-ur-jee): the body's ability to do the work of living

herd (HERD): group of animals that live and move together, often as a way of survival

hibernate (HYE-bur-nate): to go into a state of very deep sleep, where the body temperature goes down and the heart beats slowly in order to save energy

migrate (MYE-grate): regularly move according to changing seasons

survive (sur-VIVE): continue to live, in spite of dangers

Index

Websites

www.allaboutbirds.org/guide/Gray_Jay/lifehistory

www.dnr.state.mn.us/young_naturalists/snow/index.html

www.learner.org/jnorth/

www.nhptv.org/natureworks/nwep4.htm

About the Author

Julie K. Lundgren grew up near Lake Superior where she liked to muck about in the woods, pick berries, and expand her rock collection. Her interests led her to a degree in biology. She lives in Minnesota with her family.

24